The Sun

Published by Spines
ISBN: 979-8-89569-267-7

The Sun

A JOURNEY THROUGH THE ARMENIAN GENOCIDE

GEVORK DERTSAKIAN

My friends are looking for yogurt. To buy in bulk and resell. Their rationale is that it will always sell because 'man cannot live without food,' especially yogurt, if they happen to be Armenian.

I told them that man indeed lives without food, and we began to sublime into Socratic parable.

-But how can you live with no yogurt, Ara, or how can you not die if you have no yogurt? Surely, they do get their yogurt, and therefore, they do not die. Therefore, the world does not die; therefore, it is alive, and I am alive, and so makes you my friend as I know you are, as I knew you could be, as you became and continue to be full-bellied.

-Oh, Ararat, you say such foolish things. Is it to laugh at your brothers from on high? Do you not know of your ignorance? Clouded in lent on high, it grows from the mouth to the terrace and falls where neither you see me sigh. Where neither I have always been, when I was once there when you had spoken of your belly, I retained it in my memory and received it, when I heard it when you uttered it.

But Ararat did not answer. He did not speak; he did not move a learned word, not even for his youth, neither for his pressing wince, his written lips, his terrible shoulders and the idleness of his belly for which no gratitude enrolled, to his Had legs and his grateful feet, toes, which he counted in an idleness that gave him no small mercy, not even for his fellow, Adam.

So, forth Aram the Son became immersed in his sadness, in a variety of doubt, a longing for his friend, his image, his proof, without whom he thought he was to sit and no more, and, never to feel complete, he began to cry.

Aram cried, strained and embarrassed, and falling into his posture and hugging his friend, Alas, there was nothing and for nothing he cried until he knew to separate all the tears that ever fell, over every house and every husband, into all those particulars it fell, as if the rains themselves had come for their companions, the highest justice of all things counted, for six nights and seven days until it reigned, until never any province could have spoken a word.

* * *

The day was going away from Aram to be in another place. The light left the house of his friend, where it had once flushed even the poorest temples with the sight of flowers, with crowns that stood among the rays, that stood among and shone their scent, where Aram kept them in his hand, the notes remained as a string of pearls, made long by the voice on a generous heart.

The freshness left his eyes, yet the darkness set with him. The immensity of every feature set away, at first one, and then the other. Aram drifted away more than he had. Aram drifted from all things familiar, from the patience he learned at the feet of his friend, from the essence of where he counted himself among men, from the essence of the form of the earth and of men and the consciousness of knowing them, the little children who asked for much and got less, from the shelter of the apricot trees living in unreserved peace, where generous weavers died again and died every day, only to reproach and spare a moment if it came to pass, some men of solemn office who had come to worship.

Aram felt the cold in his voice. He heard the strangeness of her voice. They turned and met there where they stayed, where Aram lay; it was from him an instant longer. Beneath his breast after the waves had gathered and crest, the two figures came near at first; the companion grasped his older friend and held aloft his fellow, who stammered and blushed over his words. To be polite again was like turning to home where the jewelers repaired ships that crossed at sea and kissed their fingers easy and cleverly, that held firmest the land to the tides.

The fair stranger said to Aram:

-Do not fear, I am devoted and have given up dying, if ever you had sense, if ever you had faith that he alone knows I in the void of all things, and knowing, still, sentient Aram, to this land, long after he took their last, and for a long time was I the nearest of your friends and occupant.

* * *

Aram's intention was not to have come into the world that for him was too vast, too great an act brought to him as sudden and intense as any of his conceptions. He only wished to be numbered again; he wished to be endless again, as all those things became when they walked outward for the first time, when they took possession of the distance, when the feet felt the sudden excitement, the wonder and the pause, devoted and unapplied. Where no things profane and all advance to arrange as those things that left the ground sacredly after a length of time. This little thing of dusk, who toiled all afternoon and sat at the spot where he fell down again, where for that instant that established itself as a picture, a handsome face indeed.

Aram felt a rupture. As if he was standing before a broad fire, a career, and then an exile, whereabout he was struck and struck again. A beast, too, was all over. Shocking and intense, with the face of a man and eyes that shone like quartz that greatly held under Aram by what he did not know, his arm, his rib, his calf, cut down to his feet, and he knew this with the thick sweet air in the presence of a woman, coming nearer to the warm center whereupon he coughed and sank, and sank again, and, aware and lost as a sound of stress, He rose to say farewell, the likeness of churches and temples.

* * *

In the daydream at broad dusk, where the horizon became, where the forever preceded all that, it was saw, when the light rendered the features of the sea, the first breeze made over the water where he counted the word all the way to himself.

Aram felt that he knew where he was going, but he was going with regret, as people do when falling in love with strangers and not knowing their names. Or knowing their face. To be in love with an idea was indifferent. It did not matter if he had found himself something he did not know, as a movement that amasses great thinking and passes away.

Why does my Ararat hurt, "Mama" - for which he began his letter.

Nothing works harder than a word. It endures famine and thirst. It wants to sleep. It knows day from night, and it waits for numbers to try it twice. For her, it was his eye, and for the steady boy, it was the whole of the globe's library; for one day, she thought those fingers, those common travelers that bruised strawberries, that traced quickly in motions what were the hours when the archangel sang - dear sister you will pass, so was this zion of a new alphabet, many months high with a sleepy face.

* * *

What kind of story is this, Ara? He said, pausing and twisting his pointer finger upwards, his face depressed and misunderstood. 'These things make our whole relation so impersonal, and the shop fronts and cafes hadn't understood a word you said. It is moot, Varpet, and so what if I am Aram too, who brings their lumps with them in more languages than the native country, in the company of other men with bitter tastes just like my own, where it is said above all that fourteen years is but an eyelash. He ended his pointing. He was now intimate and confident. It's always the same thing. Many mouths that speak, from the cellar to the garret of how big a house it is, search the soul, where additions and rumors make two stories.

I'll have another coffee and plenty of it every minute so the heir can set the tables. And amid the pretty sight that is ourselves, there is the olive tree with dull complexion, heavy and good-natured, and my eyes would be too brilliant without it - I think.

And a note for our little Aram under the shade

-If I fall, I will see myself, I will meet where I excelled, and sooner than one foot is again, I am the summer. So do us earthly decedents gather, impressed by Haleb, impressed by Montparnasse, flitting together like little soldiers with two great feet that walk together. Little you move with him and never break. This story of yours is like a young maiden who didn't follow the rules of reasonable people. Go on - now that you have intercourse with the world. I have held some time wholly distinct for ourselves.

* * *

I n the hours of his youth, Aram made his room, where he knew everything had its place. Where at his bed, he knelt and dressed in the first two corners before he rose and saw the whole array.

Not knowing at first that people were so kind, he lay there on the future with arms out-stretched, and he fell into the faces, then into the eyes, then into the candles and bedsides, where every hand had found a hand.

It was in this stupor where Aram quarreled with a man, where he spoke of him, and he spoke of them and supplied a spot where life wouldn't be so full of him, where a man could escape with his guest in his pocket.

Do not be startled, Aram said to the man. I will be silent in your presence, and I will accept your words. Tell me what this rare sweet movement is that you placeth in your hand and remembereth to your mouth. This little chamber, with its exquisite rising and falling tiers and such color that I had forgotten it for azure.

Aram smiled and came closer to the man. He was a small, straight picture, round at the shoulders, with a renounced expression and a knowledge of the shadows. Aram pushed into his face and examined his eyes. They pushed through Aram with all the sharpness of a man who had been living behind him. "Go back to sleep!" The man said, showing his back to Aram, who fell long ago in a generous shadow.

* * *

G o to the music, dear little Aram, at the edge, at the window, where you had made for them a blind alley, of the apartment, where the haberdasher exchanged his impression for your company, where you strongly marked the talkers, the twenty-somethings, the mass, the fragrant people pressed upon the festive scene, and those concerned the last night with such matters that they turned round in circles. For these flowers, life had been engaged, people that you had never seen, who had stuck fast and public - a fortnight had passed, and an elder was read. In his notes, his eyes fixed on the flat of his back, seated and squared, where he gathered all his sounds, leaving one for the other in search of something that would work. Some have one son, and from them may come two, and two come three; if they were face to face, they would appear to Aram as vividly as a symbol.

That is to say to the stomach - little one, you must judge and be refined, and walk over to have a talk with those certain forms, who had been there in the morning, and now the afternoon, when their bellies felt sorry, where appetites for the news, the remarkable circus, the child that looks alone, the living the rushing the waiting all amusedly sigh and revel - have you fallen in love? And was it more than you expected that she had recognized your fall and enhanced herself with color?

Aram noticed the edge of the window, and he saw the person in life who felt the ground and everything to him, who brought with her notes from home in four lines with a little hat, a parasol - a Scottish song of her own patron. And he felt a mistake was made. That all were there, and the street looked empty, where in the idling of that song Aram asked - Do you know Ararat and what has become of him? Where the salmon-colored rays are scattered. Where he could have been a gentleman, where putting into his look was a face, supple and silent, that said to him, eat so you can become a man. Eat much and talk little.

My friend, I can see that it was delicious. Again, I can see how you could be satisfied with a dish like this, with a toss of pollock and a kettle of salacious art that familiarized us with the contents of Aram's stomach. And now I am stranded, like so many people are, here in the cafe, far from his little stomach, and I almost want to cry. I almost want to write my own story, but there is no other light than the moon dragging the table, where a heap of things strikes eight, and I am obliged to go to bed. Doubtless, I should sleep in this hovel of a night, cool only by name, for if it weren't for the delightful boy that I've never met, the garçon who has spoken in tongues, those two lovers who have all but emptied the prison for the first time, I have put aside one hundred francs to hear your story, so that we all may be rich.

* * *

Cinematic Aram, finish your talk at the woman who keeps you ignorant of terrible scenes. That keeps you in the dressing rooms, to dress your bow, so that you never miss your mass, where the heart now a mile above the church is burdened with some mist, and you are needed to lead the way, to remind us in this narrow valley the richest and most fertile with our blood. They, too, have Normandy.

They, too, had their Euphrates, out of which grew Bagram and Aghavni; perhaps you have already seen them? in their walking goatskins, working in the garden where they like to be, where they prepare a dish where there are no thieves. And Ardziv, the high tottering man. A real pest. Who at twelve o'clock plunders all the hangers-on? Garabed, the one who boasts, "You Should Have Seen That!" and Janig, who makes signs of the cross at people who are coughing and people who are dragging with bitter mouths contracted by thirst. There is Mher, who placed the black shawl over her head, and Samvel, who mingles odors and says in a low voice that he had heard of portions just beyond those walls, where there was linen pressed inside the temples.

There is Armenoughi, who would argue that there was no such semblance of this fire from fire, this steel from steel, and tier from tier, that she, the contingent world, had held for her friends, a last flame to determine her place.

There is Dzirani, who came today, just one more to round it off the third time you ask for her; ambivalent and happy, she falls on your head as quickly as she rises, with both hands out, like the sweetest of miracles.

From time to time, there is Alenoush, breathless and relieved, she reflects on the day and what you did not see, and what then you saw, with one hand to another engaged, she tired of the offertory, so she let herself go, and dropped to a seat in which confessions were made, where under her breath she sang and repeated the words of the choir. Beside her sat Ovsanna, the ever-so-modern-teenager who asks, 'Do you know the gravity of this.'

Yes, more! Aram repeated, and a little smile fell into his hand, and then another fell, paid with a smile, that newly minted and understood secret, that a young girl is a sequel to a little boy, and the two operate in this wholly instinctive business of looking after each other. Where she looked after him, and he looked after her trifles. Comrade Aram, bow-tied and businesslike, peering through the afternoon for nobody and peering again for nothing to arrive. Where a young boy and young girl consort off-stage and tryst with stolen beauties, where Aram stood at the hour of two touching, and in his pocket was more money than he didn't know. Enough to find himself on happy terms when the young girl came again to buy his leave.

For all this, Aram thought, if there ever was a restless light, it would have been a pretty day, just like yesterday and tomorrow. And Aram would have stayed over, in the presence of that Normandy, with nothing to serve, with the carnations by the Euphrates, where Baghram met, and Ardziv remained, where Garabed came together with Janig and Mher, at the table where Armenoughi remained, that passed the bread with seeds and a vision of the hostess earth, that for a kopec sprout some edible root, of middle height, and rustic hair.

And there was Aram, with his high finish, bow-tied from chin to nostril, wrapped and turning in his overcoat. Where Ovsanna asked the question, "Is it true that the Sun stood still?".

Where Ovsanna heard the question, "Did God really make the Sun stand still?". Did the sun stand as a bowtie? Might it wait? Was the ball dressed in the glass there and then? Did Joshua ask the Pharaohs first? Did Rameses consult the Cambridge researchers? Did Merneptah know geophysics? Were you caught in a well-played game? Have you sketched yourself this wild impression? She let out a laugh and, with softness, stroked his hair like a sister to brother. She separated the strands over his glance. She measured Aram to her hip, smiled, and spent in his waistcoat's pocket the last few minutes of Sunday Mass.

* * *

Concealer, Bronzer, a little bit of pencil, masquerade, lipstick, Aram thought, clinging at the alter - If he were born again, a few seconds more to wonder, as some men do, where the novel of this fair stranger stopped, after the earth was relieved, and the invisible shore in that country dress flowered in the air, where the men in two and three mixed with the orient -The Mona Lisa winced at him.

The Birth Of Venus passed his hand under her arm and drew out again.

The people stricken from this mountain current, this clean little system of curves and paths tariffed by guests. The gentlemen lingered on another night, and Aram spent away another of what he would have called a night of her life, where she threaded his shoulders a companion blanket, where she found a ragged edge to repair, where she turned back the mound with her sewing hand and made a kind triumph.

It's the smaller things that sit by the fireside. They sit there still and want things at shop windows that old friends had deserted. A pair of gloves. A glittering smile. She took dominion over all of it. What did a man's work in the world have to do with that disyllable if he wasn't in possession of it? Are you sure you are? Are you sure she is so charming in this light? The museum is just a corset. Devote another moment of adipose. Isn't her life very admirable? These remarkable fine women, she said, not a drop above twenty-two. Content with being sweetly ignored.

* * *

She accepted Aram's sleep and said to him, after all, you are the very beautiful everything when the part of the seat, the earth you owe, is simply night.

And I am thinking of you like a mother thinks of a soldier. Like a matron in a great time that pulls all things: the gust from the ocean, your letters in salt. One mark to the left. Another to the right. Beside your earliest records, the playing cards from that Virginia Company were fastened with our father's will to my breast, and I laughed. That was the size of it then.

In America, I unraveled a pretty girl and uncrossed two feet and unmoored toes, and one eye came, expecting London, and then another, and a dress that paused at all the business. And ten men walked from out the boulevard (here they called them streets) and wedged themselves in bank halls and bus stations in overcoats from yesterday. The hours came, and the cyprian icons passed under my fingers. Some sightless girls roamed with soldiers in orthogonal lines. Some manners were lost.

I let my past as a tradesman mixed with crowded figures. Iridescent streetlights melted together. I tied the loose ends of my shoes. If there ever was anything sweet, I said it with an accent as bitter as a lemon tree. I would be, I would have had, some scruples in these letters. If it weren't for our spine, we could be anything at all.

> Let me sing the sun,
> to quit his chair
> and bind these tones
> the Somme and Solent
> that hang the parts of the morning

They call it an idyl. That pause that has, like a savage, grazed your face on mine-brandishing a widow. Our house acts like the other houses and smells like bread. Our house pulls itself up to the last door and asks, 'What people do you know?' and 'Why are you here?'.

I suppose I will see the Solent Straight, Aram says, and out came the prophet to show the breakfast, sprawling from the pocket, along with all the things that gave this house a tone. Whisking in the baker's quarter, he struck land and said, 'Yes, there I am, hovering in the aftertaste, bending my laughter.'

* * *

Drink this Ara, Titian as this red air, I am grateful still, for this may have come, and I had worked around the clock today, these seeds in turn, where I speak of the best love yet, a city called Nineveh. The one that fell asleep. The one that made me fat and dressed the ship- that parted me from sailor's songs, the bow from the aft:

> It is good
> It is sweet, like me,
> to assume this passage,
> with pink lights
> When a manner quite a garment enters all.

To look for the poor in this place, my man, I should've been a Hebrew. And sat back with this companion life a makeshift smile, that in all its gaps and execrations grew words, rough and rougher, drawing in them all that it could see. My vernacular went into my eye, and into my nose hairs

the sun of my mother, my black heart and your pink panties
ironing my head, my mother-in-law, what is there-what isn't
there, had found my nose and mouth an empty barrel.

And with a snap of a finger, I called again the garçon
that had flourished and wilted, and graced again, and
disappeared. Of course, it's been an evening since I looked at
you again. The sun had lent the mountains a following
night, and another Thanksgiving when my life was fainting
away, and these bars had closed on me forever. Commune
with the Chef, my young boy. Has he heard of Jean Racine?
This fish that I have swallowed whole. The Jews come up
with everything.

Aram awake, Aram awake,
Do not be dismayed,
This sweet harvest touches your mouth.
Our country, they may say,
It is too delightful,
It is the USA

Aram awake, Aram awake,
Do not be dismayed
It is too delightful
Will you uphold thee?
Exactly left, exactly right,
They called themselves a State.

It is given to this shape,
A dreadful little thing,
Across the box, he saw his friend,
Who hung in flowered air
Exactly left, to set these bones,

Repeated two young men;
exactly right, it's working now;
they stood along again.
These Virgin Cherries touch your mouth
The Faithful Paladin,
Quiet as they closed the door,
That sounded like a hymn.

Turn your feet that giveth reason the last vestiges of the night, as a gentleman does. I hope that you have answered every little question that passes through the hills. Every discreet that collects a face, and every sudden spectator that-decorous as a windowsill-awaits the sun to come.

On boy, as pretty as a sobriquet, picking at some daisies (or was it rhododendron?). Still, Life was there, under the skin, with the Azaleas who went quickly to the comedians to tell them their patron saint had arrived. And flushed until it saw again. And the beforehand too and sat down to where your complexion came: What do people think about men wearing dresses? It's like sisters partying the night away.

I once was half your age when a minute of air had struck my knees like a dress that fell on them. Is it you that I hear, dark and heavy with streaks of red, fallen in this living room? This cheap and luminous perennial has recorded all my burdens and split between my teeth its fallen seeds.

Or was it only the street, restless with some air, to name you from the mute on the divan? I don't understand. My mother had proposed it.

* * *

You and your friend. Uninterrupted. A tiger between two trees. I thought I had thought of everything. Explain, Aram on high, how the beast had made it outdoors. I recalled that if the purpose of life was freedom, you're much too more than that. More than enough to dream. More than enough to get older. A little more to know the better from the worst. Any more than this, you warlike hang and confound the tongue, and not in that charming way that you promise to eat in the tone that the fruit grows older and falls down, past where the legions had sprung and projected their spears and had made like architects quarter-fires, where night had passed in the union of this chorus: Persia was found.

* * *

It began to rain on little Ararat and then on great Ararat and every crowded hair that had come to see the cause was stood up and plucked by the free hand. Aram cried and asked, "Where did you go?" but he was encumbered with all the things that fell on his mind, that fell some more and bound up his feet and decorated him in a row of feathers that improved him and enlarged his shoulders, and a scarce few fell upon his nose, over which he observed all the outer air, and every next comer and free thing that walked and settled. And he found the taste of those branches in his mouth that told him he was the last man sailing and to be responsible and come back on time to know me again, and his transcended companions could only laugh at what game just under the clouds were being played.

Out of there, Aram came and made over a gentlewoman seated at the park who doesn't like it over there, heard her say, and again Aram let himself go, falling luminous and course, a plume of amber to believe in.

Next, he sees a thousand bees and says these must be the people whose return is so uncertain that they have waited to see me, who talk with little bearing about the presence of me, and who work themselves around me for little benefit. And Aram fell a little lower to see her that had wandered past the others, tired and reduced she was in search of a word. She said to Aram, that she had parted once before.

You say you are not knowing the mother from the son, Aram asked, and "Yes", she replied. Do you want to marry me? I think it's called, if both of us remembered want being those things that drop into a deeper well, that I see myself with him, that presses against my eyes everything in May all the things that I have sought to know, or was it - have they forgotten me - where I had profoundly remained, where there was still so much to be said about my smile, embarrassed and full, I took to my home.

* * *

At this height, Aram thought, to even think of the sound, the one that spoke over all men and things, that had brought into him every form when he wanted to stay, that had him little by little when he had come to it, in his idleness to be just one of those stricken dumb, reared with sacred rites, embossed with those little girls who wondered whether God the Father had created all things, whether He had created them out of nothing, whether he held them out of desperation, when at first it was only sound, and it was generous and musical, and then it was a woman, who wondered why the boys were so mean, and that this one was to come and pass, and every artery would know of it.

My name is Angela, and I was panting she said to know one, and her sound welled up like this like you had heard in a girl that waited all day and then later on and 'til later on when her back was long after Aram's radiance and he was the sea, and she had repeated and climbed over him again in the acuteness of his fires, and he sunk in and tired in her making what was above now underneath, fleshed and brightened by the artist's pallet. She bent down, and what was above now she threw over Aram so far that he exactly dazzled, and he wholly believed that hidden across the sea of time, there existed those little spaces that he would know the limits of, the equilibrium of laughter that Angela knew, that held immense the sky, that she kept to herself like a medal.

* * *

Roughly, you've started the machine, and you've climbed all day asking, "What do I know?" A jealous boy that makes his steps above the orient, your face like a monster, many and beautiful. Those things, too, are no longer in the way but I won't surrender. I will wait until we both are found like this, just as we are, the last ones of two, like those brave explorers that left their fingers there I tell your part, and still, they say it was good today when the eyes and whiskers were fixed at the poles, and your companion spoke in the foreign tongue. There's our Mountain along with its legs. Doesn't it feel that way during the blue, after the red, and before the white? It turns from you to me, and you again?

Then how should we be there today, that you have

Mount Suribachi at your lips, to dry your clothes, to forget where you were among the sundries? And I will tell you, Aram, while you sit and wait, to never underestimate the enemy, because somewhere he is, holding his nakedness in front of him, guiltless and keeping the sabbath, keeping it holy and through it thunder and lightning and the mountain in smoke - I think you just saw Moses. Listen for yourself and tell the Israelites, but do not speak, or else we die. There's an altar and some burnt offerings; dress it with stones before the exodus, and in forty minutes or so, you will fit in the same clothes.

* * *

You only live for Mayflies, Aram, and today you're acting half your age; your handsome laid a trap for me, she murmured, and went back and back to find some air that fell on charming voice and said I've never had an Apricot. I brought my knife and fork. It's wisest that I pass them through this tree, to hear its last words about how it can be so good. And it said to me, "I had never seen a girl moving all alone" her eyes felt on the last century and they were honey, and they were coming within the sight of me that was already seen, and she took me again and again and I was amused, and amusing I wondered if there was ever more than one word for Egypt.

It took you eight minutes to find me, in a long night that I stood in these passages and deep gorges, this bell tower over the refectory, the mother and the illuminator stand in the kitchen with some plates and frescoes, looking back to see you in your little cries and recognitions. This could fairly be a shop window, by what breath does pass over whole, eaten and confessed and converted into life, the house the lady the work, I'm just the bleached bones of the fearful, and my hand has tired from mixing the bread.

* * *

You are in my eyes now, Ara, where I had liked to see you, and this is the last of it, my last oration. I'm so glad you do not understand. How grand to say 'he was wonderful.' And my hand was of the right stamp, if I could call it my hand. At worst, it bears with me a little Aram; at best this Moravian has brought his exiles. This one speaks of Alexandria, sumac and cumin, and dried leaves in open mouth, that's sweet, that he will pray without end, red pepper dried in the sun, the sun might make you eat, this food might make you spring, to know will make you fall, he never turns a hair, I looked for ways to read our book, peering into faces.

This one is like the foreign soil that turns up on my shore and leaves again.

* * *

How droll of me to clean your eye, but Adam insisted. What am I a maid? What am I to pick this up against this gravity and look you in the eyes? Not one of your friends takes fault, but sometimes yes, outside you go. You, you get the metal. This little cross here, this moment of resignation from when you broke out, you really showed your stuff in the palm my boy -What is your name? Wonderful. I'll remember that.

These little bosses at my feet they've sent their envoi.

Go little form, and impress to all who see these nights the fearless under the carpet, our still conscious friend, a taste of rage, a spice of wit, impressed upon me a man in defilade, the air of red youth with no relief.

I threw my hand out to the shutters and felt a pang of shame, knowing that when Aram came, dressed in black, all would be corrected.

* * *

What were we, before Aram came, I tell you Ara, it was the dark. It was the few moments that speak to me today, even if we're so full to be here, even if we have watered by our garden party, bright and extraordinary, the dark is still there, as it was, and never dies. And if you walk into that moment again, will it happen again? Will what be young but not so young talk to you again? Would it not say-never, or will it wait as I, in my disobedience, hang with such high taste? I stumble, I am ashamed, and then I am overcome. As a boy that rose from chaos, with iron in his mouth.

> My conceivable and eventful horizon,
> who rises and shows vividly the broach,
> the iris so to speak,
> that escorts ladies on a high look,
> has greeted me from the east,
> like an orthodox icon.

And if I find those apt fingers in my cake, I'll know by the good-natured wrinkles, these appended results, these lurking suspicions: Have you been stung, my dear? or is that the whole of the fat wrapped around your finger; the most fluent lies you've ever told.

We suspect you are a myth. Like a companion that has resolved to dress himself for rainfall only to find the frock, the pea coat, the brim of the top hat that says -not yet but yes it will come, it will rain cats and dogs and be led by doves who receded from the mountain and plucked at these crowns.

It was at once a glory and again an immensity, to see the child flanked by his soldier saints, gazing useless to me, gazing upward, only useless, and it was that was by design, beautiful and submissive, and if I found Aram again, arresting and handsome, I said it would take the eyes out.

* * *

Before I went away, I saw her back as it was, finding something to say with the nearest easy words that this one came late and this would hide next to this as if it were a quiet stream, in which sooner than she knew it was to gather, she never would have gathered, if i hadn't asked.

That's the thing about these mountains. They never catch their breath. They go on slabs and cowhides and hang over dinners where I find them in a camp of angels. All women think like this; it's just that some make a bad writer of it wanting to say the boy's little face and his companion's touched, or that the dinner hadn't come in time, or if the dinner wouldn't come at all, then wouldn't they be lost forever.

I kept trying to mine it. I dipped the ladle thinking of some simple expression, blessed are the young or something like that. I thought that they would rise and give me a good

day, or strike a little sooner, and rouse up the fleeting minute
when the vespers missed their carriage. All women think like
this; it's just that a better writer would have added the fat,
and backed me into the corner, and maybe some gold, where
I would fall, and kiss my nose with one more glass, knowing
if God had walked away, he'd resolve to love her by himself.

* * *

Don't pour it out anymore, Ara, this one is taking its
form, as if a fine man had found another, and having
beheld me, I am two, with either the man of the present or
of course, already that one that stings my eyes. I stoop into
the parapet and can you believe this? I swear by the light of
Mithra - "A Letter to His Lover."

It was well known that the two were held in the light of
one, and a great cook he was that seared the skin, and I want
to say like a dullard the helpless things of the lay
philosopher: It all comes from one great place, the engine,
the lightswitch, Genitor Luminis, and with a pistol shot,
Suntan has set her course.

* * *

She had in her palm a bunch of grains, and Aram could
see in the fineness of it those that swam, and he saw
that they grew, and he saw them more, and they poured out
from the sea in ones and twos, and I don't quite know which
wanted more.

Compactly held and moored these too, stupid, you'd
think, take more, know what freedom was and what it
wasn't - and they did not come. And you did not quite know

if they heard like you, because if you had spoken any bigger, of Aram and his mother, the address of the mountain, all the things to do and the so longs that follow after, the stillness and the politeness would've been dashed, and the moment that lay between the hand would have poised its head, and danced away.

* * *

Seven, eight, nine - Aram counted all to himself and fought the urge to fall asleep, and brushing the dusk, he made himself straight again and brought to her all that be there, those moments when the appeal to other fingers - ready or not - had been exhausted.

Don't worry, in an hour or so, your song comes on, who lied and ate his food and yes, who lied to lie with me, and to come back to the people with a message of hope, a small light that had no wish to look or speak. This Spanish nun, exquisite and finer than porcelain lodged in the cedar - worked to make herself this charming creature and to give herself a crest when Aram came: To be alone and not alone was to watch the sun parade.

What's the matter young man? Do you need a lantern young man? That being that planted me from whom I wander, to obscure myself and make myself this small deal, does he look upon me now with no concern? Surely not. I too, would look for myself too, if I did despair, if I was creature and if I was creatured, naked and bejeweled, poor or rich, you'd find me on a plate of gold.

* * *

It was the hour of profuse sweat and Aram felt that she had liked him, and he had felt it too, although he could never be sure. In the day time, the park was, after the last winter, warm and dry.

When the spring came, they believed they could outrun the clouds, not because they were tempting fate, but only to look back and see the rain for everyone. The slim dress clung to her hips. Her hair had curled. Her hands unclasped into his as he kindly interrupted. The streets had taken on a breath of ash and lilac through the nostrils. The madams found an easy awning. A newspaper was carried. The windows streaked with the old and young having it out.

Fate was not - youth going now with Aram to grow up. It was all that happened, divided and pitched, as that sense, one would feel after a sudden darkness of the rain that came from it. Cubits she thought to herself, smoothing out the wiry curls her mother had picked for her. The radio said three hundred cubits or something like that. And some Gopher Wood, and my God, my dress is wet. And thirty cubits in twos and threes, how do they fit all stacked up on top of each other like that. Perhaps it was an exhibition. Like that circus that came, and he took the girl off right at the hips as I watched it, and side by side she was, whereupon our friend recounted the sweet foreignness.

And fifty more cubits and behind me was the cavalry, these curls went into waves and the waves had struck and fallen straight.

Fearless it is to go out without a parasol. I only say this for myself. The rain is not for everyone.

* * *

Armen, my body, you don't mean to fall, over and under and pull. You taught me with this braided cheese the village of honey and olive songs, in the room of the house window and sun, and cloud borne flesh and fat from the god, and yogurt met from lemon and thymes, that made a bow and came inside.

Anyhow I give you Aram, washed and absorbed the goings on, collar undone, unbuttoned and spread like a flood, the face a cupful taking your name in vain. And here's my sock, if there is any use for it. Perhaps you'll settle in and read me this stupid book, full of absorbing materials. Written to the eleventh letter, it sounds like this: Lamb we are keeping, the meat we are eating, honest and clean from the stores we don't go. Wishing you goodbye with the wind. Smoking, it's a harm to my health, I beg you.

Teach me how to read it, the super nova. It was almost everything before I left school. I would go to the amusement park in the low of the night, and much to myself I met the years this way. It brought to me a rush as one would get when they yelled at me to stand up straight, and right away I was a man, picked up and esquired, and with not a waste of soap I counseled each hair that I plucked from its home. And then I washed my hands. And I knew what was the matter, and I knew it was impossible to be late. I knew time and I had lengthened my brow. I forgot each grain of hair into the sink as I remembered myself in the Fall, like the sun that stood out on its walls, provoked to grow more and more like a beautiful child, I give you nineteen hundred and fifteen if you would receive her, as the sun disk that bleeds away, gathered from her mother's back shadows that were long, and these letters with their arms held wide find me like a sound, and dwindle from the high trees, the cries disappear, and I thought you could do anything into the world, even on the back of tea leaves you could do anything in the world, you could right anything in the world.

* * *

The first day was sweet as gold. Looking for an ink to write this ode, if I offended peace and defended war if I had more in my heart to say, it broke in my hand as well as you kept it. Would you read it once and never repeat it, the pirate that had separated, that writes of chocolates and blades of grass and plumes on a disordered map a desperate bird that mimes all day, an adventure that is over there?

And so is Aram with a sword, is all the things that candles make, schoolmates and Geneva kings, and teardrops that stand on ends.

Sweet escape. I thought you said that you loved me. There's nothing new, yet you found me, and I have never seen the like or a parent that said yes, like the parchment at the end of winter, the mountain looks today.

Real bright, you would say for chocolate, and look over those hills: not dazzling, not the most of the night, not the race or the vagueness. They don't look like much; some chattering wooden buckets, women that mule water, that strike the dust off hides and make confessions, and confident girls with eyes of all colors, a face full of eyes where apricots and French grains would have been laid, closer to the mountain a cloud with one island, and all the saints that gathered around it.

You can have all of this. Every day without a doubt. It's certainly yours and take mine too.

* * *

I've seen it before, Ara, the sun has two tongues, not one before the other, and makes a show of his welcome. I am dumb when we encounter in the morning, doubting my hands and what is in between them, and I keep explaining, and I draw on what's before me, lured from today, wandering on to meet the younger thing.

My hurry has the sound of a room that one mentions if they had appeared there only briefly, when they mystified me and took my coat, in the ball of the ballroom, with a thousand little mirrors all on myself, faultless in this mark of night, the grandest nature of the littlest child I took to myself, and compared it to the dolls.

Dream on me, all knowing pupil, to which we promptly undid our mouths to say anyone but her, is there anyone else, but like a yarn from me she continued her sleep that breathed a good mother on its calfs that said the next thing was nothing, white and quartered alive.

Pity me and I will speak a dozen hours the first words that dream on me, that name a new place, grass eating sounds and irregular things.

* * *

You wouldn't think much of my dress today, you wouldn't think much of it if you saw it, you'd pass right by it, you'd manage without it, like a thought that had escaped you, that left its tail outside the door, and restless you made no sound, like an old house that you intensely looked at, with its large doorway and high ceiling, and its long steps behind you, isn't it, like rumors of your first kiss, with no peace between the next one.

It's already wrapped up, I thought to myself, it's fine the way it is, and I thought of its color, like an emerald or something restless in the night, the northern star was just to look at, the courtyard was for lovers, and burning was you compared me to the fools, and what a scene it was, that if you had turned it upside down, when Joseph held the sun and moon and a band of light, and socks inside my vale, heavy to the earth and leven to the stars, like the son that wanders in the field, I uncovered like a revelation, I left it to tell yourself to keep it there, devouring and smoldered, because running into you again was like watching the sun writhe.

* * *

These Three Dots, these medallions, red and white while my eyes turn, not knowing that I knew myself the way the mountain had known me, the way sometimes I had thought, when the least was the most of you, when I seemed at the very outset as I was with you, and you were few of me, like my mule that walked himself until he couldn't, and I guessed that was his manner to be that way, to be bread from his instincts, what need was there for that, as the legend says, there was a silkworm with two hearts that laid a web at the wolves that were coming for it, and he took the gauze and made every echo of what he thought he clung to, and bright stripes for what the world impressed on the edges, and ornaments and relics that hung all over, and the fancy people in America that mounted it on their cabinets, and stood there in brass and faces that passed under a sun that was not moved, that just fell again, the wolf into his father's line the objects that had parted, and the beautiful that shall not pass indeed is what I sewed of it, and I compared it to a silkworm, and I felt a prayer that asked if there were greater ones and the mountain gave me pressure, and I felt my place, and I knew it about you, like the woman that did not have to prick her finger to know it was America, the mountain of it indeed when I was sewing, that let it grow over my wine and my shoulders, and stood there on the lake and on beaches as the tide pulled the shores, or wherever the case might be.

I never felt that I should sacrifice or be called eccentric. That was my personal view. I was keeping time with Aram.

* * *

Look at this lavish banquet, Ara, you might have guessed it was all mine, as you thought of nostalgic men, nearest and furthest that speak rightly, and in their left hand the tabula the result of small reminders like your mother, who even if she had no name would have picked the oldest grape leaf, from a time before names, from the nearest heir of the plot of land, where 'where have you been' was asked as if it went to face its dreams, and upon awakening had forgotten to name them'.

I live this life as I remember dreams, a quiet spot that is ready for me, that shows itself at the moment of supremeness, this Mesopotamian, this Sicilian, this Persian that was my idea, that I took at your expense, like the sun that went down from the banks to live in debt - I ran into these grape leaves, and I fell into her fingers, and all the things together, like the son that waits for the bell, and forms

at her back and breathes in her shawl, I have become
accustomed as they say, to just chew This One Thing, The
name of things with roots, and narrow streets that lead to
theaters, I rise from my garden to my sofa inscribed with no
sense, only the want to see my house again, inscribed with no
sense I said, like a heart that ceased to beat, like a woman that
gathers all things that bore I take the rains, and my nose it
breaks the fall.

* * *

You can count on me son, you can count on me, over
hearts that ceased to beat, that is, to the bottom of it
all, that was your fingers turning rare, and turning quarters
into kings, and taking notice, that life changes very little,
even for a boy.

> I want to know what wisdom is the envoy on
> the carpet
> and all the things that are written on it
> the keys you lost and recollections
> and worries on the table
> and lemon colored days that I'm obliged to
> father over
> and I want to say that something's done but
> the rival was heavy and he began to
> count the hours
> as one book atop the other.

I might as well have plotted stars, and kept them for
review, to keep them for my wisdom, to count again and to
be younger, to touch every pebble of star and sit it on your

knee, as if it were never read, like the first man that waited the sun. It is the third day of wisdom, and engraved in the morning he wagers of the trees, and the seas and grass and fruits, whose seed was in itself after his kind, and he saw that it was good.

* * *

I waited for the sun and for Aram to ask about your health, and I remembered in my confusion to count your teeth, which you do.

Your little song is a pain in its mother,
who afterward, took with his own hand spots of water
to grow it on its own,
your belly out, and all of it is swollen,
that if asked to come, it would laugh and say why should I?
It is my life's work,
it was found somewhere in my life just now, to you,
with a number that read "Nothing in the following will
frighten you," and indeed it never did
but lay claim to the end of profanities,
where the truth was all kept or expunged,
with a denouement that says, 'Lay your belly just right
there.'
kiss Napoleon with history,
philander with Socrates,
meander with the Sun King for water with your horse,
only to find a dried-up river
or a Martian surface that longs your name,
and speaks it in small bites and replies to me with anything,
anything, mother

but just not that.

* * *

Today was not a day to ask for you, or to ask for supper, not on the floor, not at a second glance, or all the things I thought dead to stand on their cars again, to have two hands and to take part in the deep and give it again, and be made at least quite again behind me.

I thought there was pleasure in your art. That you would set it on fire for disobeying me, and from the low the charred tides leave to take a seat and then to rise, like light that comes from windows at a distance, you grow into the home, a strong man I said simply, believing in what you do, expecting your indifference and giving it.

This is a profound feeling
Getting on with me that is.
Shaking off the menace that says I am moreover my ideas are extravagant,
you will learn as much as you wish,
you will be uneasy as much as you are thrilled, you will feel despite the business.
You felt in you all the spite of all the courageous,
the vulcans and the metal smiths, the strife and the thrill of all of her, all the risk,
all that was not your idea,
all that was jealousy,
that had parted ways and pressed into the foot prints just the world, to make sure if you were absolutely bothered,
if you were understood for a moment,
you would be civil to your mother who said to him -

you are a grown man now,
imbibed with all the streams of thought,
tremendous and just to all.
But what did it matter to the dead that seemed it. Clearly it
was no trouble.
Still it sits against me, Ara, the boy a conscious man, from
what an empire cross the stream,
by what matter,
by what unbroken clasp is this a happy life,
to mean that as he is,
a prophet by the mass of things written in your book.
I mean that as it was,
like the sound of a laugh I trust the day before it smiled
and came tremendous,
so that all of the wildlife and the hands that turn in water say
in me, do you like this warm hat,
do you like to write this winter in unbroken lines?
Still, deep Aram, in your own momentum lie, like those that
clasp their hands upon a thing, a little world inside a splash
with relics and old letters,
should say to me that such was the library of Tigris, rich and
course with us and black is still with blue as the mountain
with myself,
fixed upon the morning
and began to yawn and see your face,
and the little bags that took their time and said to me
hold out your hand and give myself a thing of you,
and skip it off my knee and off my fingers,
onto my brother,
onto the mantlepiece the embers between my lady's legs, the
sun, the off sun,
I lower my voice and take another handful, and laugh again.

I was late for work today,
so that I could share a day as you
do abrupt -
like a child that asks 'how much do you like',
and that is all of them with her face before yours,
shaking as the first words 'I like you',
I'm ready to fall now,
and draw a breath of courage from the strike that says
I am brave I said,
I am little I assented,
and I brought with me my knee so that you will have your
little patience.
But with you, Aram, everything had to be shared, everything
I could do that here
I am a fortune,
coming to the garden,
pursued by a break with saying I am not destroyed,
I wait for the fire,
I wait for your heart on it like years, like an arrow that sings:
I have seen all these girls in their extraordinary things,
perhaps mayn't I have had one for myself?
if only for the trifle of work,
if only itwas torn out and given
up its freedom,
if I had went - straight on,
as that one that in the light,
that if you had met it - it would be so charmed, immediate
and beautiful,
and questioned and wasted,
and seen you was to found myself,
in the air of your lungs,
exclaiming and aching.

And what about this Ara, what is it about this old lady,
as if from the apex,
when all the things that did bear from the deep smiled upon
the top, to know when you see it - my friend they call it
strength,
or before strange I took you from bad memory.
What is it to age my friend?
To feel the blood on your cheek and to give the son away,
like two arms that broke the tide between the ships,
and took their forms,
the youth in their young say a faux pas like whatever in
America, I'll get back to it,
I'm on the verge of an old world, vivid as it grows in my ears,
my skin opens to this woman
and out of it had been a world as wide as this grand way.
I can only take a breath,
I can only add one moment
to confront it to the next and say each day after all was gone
is stranger than the veins in me,
and what my mother believed,
or what she called these burning sores are hard to close, as if
they had insisted and had lived and it was over,
as simple as a truth could be,
As a mother of a sun, as a mother of a son,
under this slight harshness of the bastille doorway
it leaves all things,
to tell you clearly about the US, the Son and her daughter,
the op-era glasses,
hands shaking at the casm,
from the theatre to the street exclaiming take her to America
and repeating it,
and rising from the perches I like her too much,

tender and awkward and tone deaf baboons,
you don't think I have seen it, on my back, I have seen it.
Grab hold.
I'll save you, if I can.
I try to come with rain Ara,
yet my tirade is broken,
that come an artful night
the crazy and the mad cows that choose to want to remain,
to listen and let me try him,
from the boudoir of my window's edge
or the minutes and numbers small that it was known that
you sing and sing of spirit guns,
and cry with your men for mullah
kid for kid yearning yea and no
My Father's Sun that is
something to peer down on,
the perfect weather for misery
that I say this with a straight face,
that you'll have to be, to come up, with the lark,
to the sun and what it does,
such as to say, she sings, after who you are and take my seat
And there you'll feel, the songs of according the world in the
present
The wolf, the place of where from which the people draw, a
symphony of suns that want us to know,
that if we had you ever smiled with a frown,
that this nature is we talk today.
Teeming with a woman
who chose to be,
and talk further of your eye,
and if there is a place of flowers as well the weather breaks it.
This unfortunate universe

that so blandly falls on us that moves and endures,
that doesn't say that it is so close,
and seizes and cuts
and words and pleasure movable as music,
what do we call her,
magicians and their tampered worlds and their solutions.
The sun is difficult to say than what I wasn't to say about its
Rose, That is for another lictor,
Now back to the months, back to the weather,
Do you see it?
A little twist of reddish hair, do you see it?
Do you need much of the birds after that, if they sing on
their own
when they create their song,
of the Son and his woman,
in the light I suppose.
But mine,
long legs resting on the flaws of arms
in fury,
Among the red of that service,
that masks the small of my lacquered corpse
Indicated scoundrel,
it's just me in here, the black with the blue collar I am
here and Iago for the duration.
personae me, one over the other, the breath of small foul
autumn Travelling through the 'morn
But tis a bleet,
the color of morning dew that flees a child
Yes it's mine and all mine,
I am that which parlays beneath the wind,
and speaks of the dam'd earth
through which the number four

is scorned and on call,
repressed as the sound of a clarion, a terminal spring,
fleeting as a fugitive,
hiding adonai,
smart and pensive as all who thought of earth
and one moment while I am working, as I pass over the seeds
lass among the sky's deep blue I waited
aqueous as a chaff-ed spirit Wild as a destroyer
aspirated by all that knows and revolves around the score
I, like sugar,
so much to say for girl l'atre meson close,
yet i have heard
that when the air surged Vaunted as a passing army I
remained as all truth
that kept me in it night
there are dreams that sit, deserted as a lulling boy that shares
a vision tantric as a color
in milk white
The sun and flowers grow as if I waited
In thy voice,
oceans lie the first palace, simple as an always
that taught the note of I Encouraged to sleep, discouraged to
be awake, towers over they to
Lift me in the wave
And heavy as the honors that were thine,
I think like kings and prance with
angels,
And lean on those tho no'ed
not the grand of night,
Striving as they once did
a path that paves of gold, curved upon me like a pulse,
wanting and stricken,

lower than a spirit
Born in verse all the all the i extinguished that I wake
If only the winter come,
To pant with me I'd strip the sky and spoil all the ocean
To call you mine again
Repair-ed only once
as the sequence of the planets did rough to tell me no,
these are not doves
and neither do they fly
as certain as they pass
off to war
in désolé I decay
the scatter at the first
the time unto this canto
waits for who should love it first that grows upon the me
and you,
Let us come together
Willingly and scattered,
Sad and happy as I commence Like a fugitive
as form did lye
Impetuous as a bed of water
inert and longer than an echo
fallen from the mark
hunting or
perilous and foul
spilling in the valleys
in roars and shakes upon the granites
and you,
my willing,
flee and stay with thee
in pose and call
as all that true

as all that take their score
When the sun that rides the valley grows simple and
incredulous
as a sound lost to heard again
the earth awakes
and as for my triumph born to pine away
as the pensive stones in fortes
that castle the terrace Wait within the new
I was at once that tall, when i fell afoul of thee My Trajan!
my good hello
and flesh within my ben chi' v'
I receive into the infernal found within a yellow flower
the greyest sounds
of farewell to me
I pursue
An image of my daughter The Sun and Moon alike that
grows within my folds
In my grief,
I speak upon the saints
and grew into the gods
the sun revolved the plains
I roiled within my grief
and felled into the small
and remained there unto death like wealth,
a poor man that for nothing sought to shelter me
from all that pines away
- at once I loved you
neither the vastness of the sea nor the sonnets of
the fall
not a long way the ascent upon the mountain,
I cast upon my cry
aloud,

Quivered upon the vision of the day I march upon this
vested wall
for water for myself
Alas! in all the things were found The mind of god
Devoured by my worth
my comrade you are sweeter than the globe
as all the things were found
the violet make-ed in my breast Admired by its master
Come and let us lye,
Let us roam between the moon, and know within thy fear,
no otherwise than us
tameless as the form of man in wandering our heaven
I Fall upon the thorn
For clothes upon my breast I pale like fire in your eye and
ride upon the wave
swift and tame
I spread upon the tangled earth I bloom upon the chains
Refuse it,
To give in that is,
snow that pants on fires
and falls nebulous as my sentiment
Profound as a memory
I consult my cure without a lyric.
dear light, this is all of what that is
happen before me as the nymphs escape.
For if it was worn it would talk of this: Lungs and the theme
of lungs. Infiniti.
And have I said that I hate kings
Have I.. Then I have and let me speak no more
of their sobs and of a pundit that spoke of no more of
walking backwards.
like you I wince deaf of it

Deaf of my deafness
I fall upon the dogs of satur Spill'd as the August
light walks upon me like a sob.
And again I have kings And still a nymph escape
Happy at this second solace
This gloated runs with me like furrowed brows Plush'd with
stately gowns of red
fond and broken
like the texture of a woman stole
I am crowned with legs as my soul to goodbye and hello
grows within this alcove
And yet I don't have kings that nymphs escape me and
refuse it in the snow again
the fire that pants
coital as it falls
I hope to know of man that groans as a tremor in my feet
The Abbasid taught me fierce in sleep To walk as I demand
And run upon the air
as the sapling in the dark stood still
Dear light yet I refuse it
As a nymph escapes a king,
I am stamped with no more hope
than what a turquoise would have glint for me
As a tremor lives with me,
this gloated runs with me like furrowed brow For is all that
talk of beasts
I speak as if I walked away
Yet I run upon the air
and consult my cure without a lyric
By chance I have the kings
in knowing that a nymph beholds me,
I molt upon the earth in stanzas

held captive striking noise
like the feet of doves
that prod at the piano
I speak of infinity and profound at nothing of it.
Yet I speak of Kings,
And the nymph behold me
I am crowned with arms and my heart it grows the alcove
I speak some more of walking backwards,
But the tall is all that was,
Stamped with light
the sapling holds a dove upon the mountain I tremor at its
feet,
stolen from my second solace,
I run under its gowns a textured
woman
I wince at the deafness of it
Spill'd as the august sun
The sobs that fall upon me without lyric
I speak upon my nymph, the light it crowns my spirit the
beating of my eyes,
this gloated runs with me a stolen woman. Glinting at my
turquoise,
The red of kings by chance
profound at nothing,
I spill,
long into infinity and refuse it,
Over and over again into abundance,
I fall upon the dogs of satur
The light it walks upon me like a sob.
Anonymous Love Letter
A man who tries to not be poetry, For who are we
That work that we are to be cured without my fingers

For who am I,
for years from now I find no reason in the slums
and in the bears
of temperate dirt
and having taken breath
my beginning that endeth within the growing of the night
the figure of my lips
long'd as the shock of flesh perched upon my form
Like a native in its first soil
This is a fortune I have yet to bear
I am taken into brother's hands, And at first I am delighted,
to be asked in what I do
is to be the rise of noble kinsmen
I arouse the ardor
I draw upon the cause of sleep
I claw upon the feet of names
the dust within that falls upon the rain, and calls upon the
father,
my joy is thrown from its convene hands had lost its collar,
and courts with me a house of flies
Heaven is to judge,
the region la fiumana ove
by the act of god I dare not say and therefor plead you this:
if honor were thou mine,
-if there the walls were taunted, and howl upon a
brigantine
I marvel at the sound of light
I starve upon my neck,
Like stars upon that lose their dusk I lift upon my voice
Whereupon I ask you this,
If the sun came upon me
in the morning

To live upon another day would it siren within the matter no
more than is my sire of you
And still I've lost my wits
For where are we to talk of you,
that spread under the cities
and March upon the seeming chance, I count my price
inside my sleeve
that haunts among the plains
The bells of daws to peck the voice I charge into my fate
I break the wave
-a ship evades the ocean,
my pride it rests
in battle dress
could have no greater place to crest.
My way that I fell upon the love of money
mischievous as a blood hound
to have been hoisted upon the world, I thought upon the
color of my knees, and of elbow joints,
and then I laughed at me.
Never could have I
wholly known
That I had looked upon a thief
On my thoughts of something first, whether it was supple
that if a mark has passed
the love of a man to know himself from you
two poems
for the one that stole my wallet, and another
dormant,
Where had I elbowed
and a thought that plundered, I walk upon the upright
And what is good
will the sun have do

profound as modern cars
a pendant cross,
I run a cette croyance
and what is left
Idle as all of all incorrigible
nature all of nature
would conduct itself against a volley, And render like the
sleep of fall
all of the churches
I chant upon and bristle at my god
If the balance
of my life
Was held upon this mountain
as a bandolier upholds a woman that says etait tempts men
or boys I drink upon a holy roman ghost that still arrived,
tough and raging
as a thought under my skin
it gave me man
and all of reason,
to yoke and pine
lovely as my youth was knit I revolt along my violet spine
I am blood,
I am merely called to be an air
And to never know
that I followed you to war
and grew my beard for you,
as a round that stands profound in fluid air, The things that
sleep in me,
And illuminate my hair and eyes And flex within my hide,
I charge into the lightning,
And fold that all that had commenced before me, Like a
river that fords into the desert,

I arrive upon the rails,
And fill my purse with money
Thou art made of me
fair and full of reason,
I have told you often
of the men that passed
Je m' Endors and Edmunds, That stood over my iris
and counted all my foals,
And found no more of color
than my pleasure look no further
we are in the morning,
we are in my bedtimes,
As a rifle fare that cracked the swell of sound, plum'd away
the time before the first;
I have not changed
I am still of you,
again and again,
as a price that crowns
I've gone to sell my land
In my strain I campaign within
that I will keep the past
what drinkest thou,
I ask with tethered voice upon the water
all the weeds that had been sown, before its kind that years
in imitations the excited would regret had come and gone,
had pull'd all away from me the balance of my life,
the cooling of my age,
my most pretentious heart, To pour me the taste
of infant honey,
that I exist
reposed,
Detached and stationed

as a love that is free of cause of all cause,
that when I arrive,
this sect that fights not one more of the idleness of life, not
even the basest,
not even nothing manicured to stand in nothing
but the perceive'ed minutes
supple and asleep,
like the color of flamingos.
My love is in this camera
there are, Romans in this thing,
That come apart with in me light the last we spoke I asked of
money I came thee often and left again the unwound of
time,
this is more
cheap and domestic
I trot amid a glint you change - intern in me
a cause to stars endure
that drown
in opals and guards the trove I sit
in livid and in dance'd
to rejoin along
thy pulse
I love thee more
How happy am I that you are come as a River that abandons
none
I rest apart with words to make a man
obscure that dive
in the ballad of the morning,
driest as a burning nettle,
I reproach at time
that caught within its ship
the ballast,

I damn myself
to plunge in suns that sweat
that mate at long last sweat that pours like wine along my
fingers
The sun it sleeps in all its industry, compass'd by its lasting
mountain, wilt betwixt
wilt my chariot,
to jostle in thy chamber
and prolong the ember part of night
the instant of the two found man,
and given to the living hues
the reason to be cruel
to be thus the rail that grace
the furs that worn the fine destroyed upon my head,
thou dirge,
thou turbid cause of man,
- I would laugh
if love was not the dying of the year,
it cannot be said,
the Venetian had enjoyed
- continue her
my violet pour in question mov'd extant rather fall the
clouds extinguish all of man
than exchange my sister
in her womb
carry on,
the light of greatest bow,
is here again,
the cossack locks
the cross that yields,
I poise in all the fields and call it love,
I gallant in the rage of cooling rivers,

I study all your names
A race from mane to tails
as held the sky the sun that cups I art as thy new kingdom
my servant of the cause, fastened to the spill
the ragged man that scarce belongs,
I spire like an orchid open -
I confess upon a friend
a corpse amid the lairs,
I found and never dumb
the sweetest scales of reason
There were Romans in this thing once upon their shell This
Thing that tempted crossings
and reflected of pendants
that never loved thee after,
That never knew the semblance,
That only grandest chapels
had they run away and chanted
in the first,
spread upon the chaliced angels, tangled in the crowns of
castles, laying in their heights the breath of August.
If i could ever see unsaid my youth again
the leaves undead my driven spear as white as snow
That come apart with me in light.
my finest hour
shall i go home now under my hand
I wrote
shall good my soul immersed in given day to perfume reveal
my semblance
like the coming of hello
why should I
my tongue what pen for not with both firm legs
the ragged vines that rise

a thought
that breaks
the tides that node
that tide amid the snout of bears indeed my words are ghost
that love of loss
I speak to where the sun would rise
if he were the more to lodge with me
Goodbye for sport, I leave to grow
to pick
the very finest eye, myself a bride,
the heart that fall
my question curl of lips I read me there are you
much longer than before
I wait for blood to turn as if I bit the light in pride to shine
the pride at rest
to call you grief
hello to you when once you were the form of grace,
Again I lie with you,
a thousand days I walked apart behind my words,
what we do is grave
what we do as a mountaineer that bucks the office chair,
and chides to speak of glory and the color of strong things
compared to boys
that pirate globe
the grandest first after the opus
the pendant joined along the hip
I'd rather stay
I am cruel and absorbed with fate absorbed amount my
palms
I hold a key,
Too heavy or two glorious
to laugh at the heaviest of sounds understood as song

perhaps a whisper,
please
as thin as air
You approach with lungs for me, I animate and pull some
book further from my breast,
one day I will have instruction for us both,
just as I said,
what I never wrote,
and made happy
and dumb for not a reason
known at all,
as the air that leaves the mouth of doors,
I only gawk,
and only see,
I listen to your tones,
I could never be
different again
that I know each from other as the mountains having met,
my name was written in my mane, I follow prey and mate
and father litters
I stride upon the hide
and slash the question virtue from its very beard,
I wear upon the very granite
and make a purse of it,
as the gravity usurps the water I fall into the night
with madness for my hands,
that draw upon the smallest light or the greatest, alike,
for what the deeds of fathers,
I majesty the tongue
I follow and I brag
I take and make a gentle mark, as a feather in my hand
the swords of Macedonians

My Theatre
in my jest you heave me forth the fullness of forgot
I ask a quarter charles
how dare the noble white that rhymed,
thinkest any more the sun to daughter me in heat
to box,
to never look back upon it, without a prayer or smile
that sit upon a wish
with dearth
amount the mount have give me more
than I forgot,
more than was my tongue,
my heart and eye as one
That hands my free to you that lead
come noble film
or woman pole,
consorted all the youth of vigor life at rest,
as you had said
that tiresome
was I, that tired and blink
the merry clothes that drape the patterned morning
I snap and hope
with all the false bravado fall set and pale the lead the night
that shine,
the air that sit
the love abate
to yield at first we met
Hello abrupt and good the 'morn, it almost is,
if it were to wait the longer,
it if were to hand me time
as if
a coin that fell

had come upon meridians flat
the gentle man of me
the clang of armour
not ever did it sparkle
a diamond pale
the man that won and had the field that charged
had cut
obtuse in all
the matter fit my hand
thou knowest me
from a lame that ride the torrent morn'
and walk at certain pace
to prove the might
that send a question
rust as wilted autumn
I am revenge,
and man that go to sleep
to pause and wait at master's step the honor will be mine,
as veins are sure to wilt
flushed with me this act we set beneath the stars and laugh
within a chamber
made,
as hearts that beast
were red as they were white,
the washing of our hands amid our fate
no more than would I eat if I were cold,
you ask if I am rich,
if I am healed it would be one
a number call that had within my grave impressed a savage
grace
gentle is the stillest night that gave me name,
and fold upon my sheets it ran my palms

an order that would fall my sound
my dearest come the somme levant and grant me this allure
a dormant fire
that formed in myron's granite eyes the object of my flight
anything for you this act
it was the third
to question pinch my sleeve, for if I awake
would follow into life itself your idle blush
if only you would sleep
latin brute awoken
all the child
allure in heavy tongues The drawl of wav'd armies,
drink upon the Gallic walls
the fullness of their armour,
if eternal had they heard the isle that many years had passed,
forgotten man itself,
the mountain's flesh that part the rows of valleys,
that flowered with the stag
and may I ask,
in part that you were very reason scales that blister all
restraint,
the face of god
and dinner tables
furnished 'pon the brows
the latest of the middle tongue,
the wading of the tongue in air,
the slightest sound that wait on call that wait and lie in
darkness flat and flex and wake thine eyes
that strike upon a king their lines, like fat upon the chessman
wait
you roam my king in art uncompromised in color, art thy air,
as grain reflect

I satellite
the married templars gate,
I disparage and confound
at the poise that sun's had held in widow's wise to never ask
again
you lower brow
to cleaner path,
the baron speaks of worlds
awash
under thy feet had known of lesser mount
sunder thy delight
a noble hoove,
Withstood a noble calf,
I waiteth for the light of day to hollow art my love,
hello again, the rise it was all that
about you wait, with hands that clasped the flect of trinit
branches
loathed as a color
unexact that breatheth
inexplicable
from where the arm of winter
cast
I welcome back, the roses mired sunny caste
and flower child,
what game was I that cov'd placid roll of water rome
I brought it into nothing,
as an anchor holds the shole admired boat
what song was this that wrote without a roll of white
that
return again the flight of all
that undulates the whale of maps the origin

of cities hide in harbors where the naval hearths the ardors of
the jealous
fell,
to indicate the promenade
of sounds alert the fort upon thy dove
I speak and never stop, I follow
foolish art of cheaper merchant's venus naked lies,
the wave again
the mountain and the sun
that earthen jewels had strung
you saw the peaks that took their form,
may tomorrow hold you placed,
the number turn transfix the fleet of blackest legion,
in my very flight,
I write bout the see
the time it made to wade,
to hold unto the brow the
clouded days that sail
and never fall.
This chapter called The Gloom of sending towers, fell once
again the candid light
understood
and wept
the sun has two paths left my friend,
that brought upon our might a name
from which there could have yours to speak
a writer
had they grown
they would
have rode the past
that held us what

difficult world unfolded off the magnet's more of minute's
friend I am to you
let us abandon
youth
by minute loss of found
our kin by sonor eye
by call of I that eat of fits of old
to have by god the mountain sour
more on this as news had come like forest breath,
the leopard lost in bitter land, comply thy hide
compass had asked by violent black had drowned my breath
my sated life
upward to test
to noon thy carnal bound
simple heat can not recall or reach by it
profess'd call to wilt
May I
be given Reach
for Thou are as the emblem Ride my nail
as if they grow with further sound
I wait purview of all to perfect
the thought of thy
to write in water black as fall
to rise like smile indeed have I
The question asked the more the call by change of you
thy love me for
if prophecy had
project to further eye the goal
the man that folds the bow
of captain's ride
the foals of autumn's rise
like question of the sun to wilt

they do and faulted as a brother's blister
black as blue had called on atoms
locust
all that left the folds of pearl
the cousin might the founder of the red that wilts
the gentle Newly girls that bide had given quill
portend and fine it is
but more that follow on
and swell thy merely sect
This blood
this cut of thing the book of author's mark that knew and
yet a bitter nerve
it was
lost and tumble
tongue
it is but nine
The birds that flew could tell
But stupid mother calls your name
I found you there in sands of poets' Persian grain,
with coffee twills
I make you mine,
invited into salty bastions,
And labyrinths to give you color
held there before naked bath
I civilize and ornate time
it grows amid the gown of thee
the gold and wine
the incant crows of creole words
that pass like soldier's writing daughters back of letters home
the clips'd sun
May we have one more my love
Of sitting as those manic ornate cloves of glass had made,

congealed my fall
the cough my dowry work across
of simple men that sneeze
into their woodland hand
thy father's oak,
The rain it fell again the color
had returned,
like knees that arc the weary earth inside the morning glow
the private heart of greener ferns
I never give,
I quicken at the furthest earth
To quench thy lips
the tumult of fleeting ash of dire's
greatest river
held the rains your truest gasp
Your Man Your Horse the finer sword you gave me home,
you hid my beard
So far behind.
my friend here is,
The breath of morning song fluoresc'd suns
That differ frame
and bear the lock,
Protrude in open plane
the parse of ears
of flag and banners raged, the oddities of smile
of foreign faces lay
the sparkled hand grenades,
and take with me this note the hour come
confus'd youth
that give
upon the stars
their very pause

to gain for moment's
pose the measure readeth I

* * *

In second's path the measure stands,
My lonesome grow
it test the time,
more handsome than a warring partner, learn'ed all its words
the greater smile, I come to you,
in bleach'd sounds of speaking bones Imbibed with light,
In arms with highest eyes
the universe
would it convulse'd
Sparks and ashes
worn with me its colored socks
I smile at funny things,
so in love with the new purpose I have found, Like trails that
mark their paths in forest contrails, where even if I took
with me
All the thought
that curious feet had ambulated,
the date of Emma,
idle as the shyest friend that wait for me
The sun's divide,
My only said
we meet again,
if the days add up,
and prod your mother, this replicant
with glittered iron
speaks of gold,
The Alchemist its virtue rolls,

I change for you this wood and marble,
and flowers for your colors marvel, and photos of the
cavalcade
and sugared water
For flavors noted in your tonsils,
let's talk about the wounds Of time
As if I waited,
in the very room itself
In them you wandered Dryer than a trabador -
I'm sorry
is this an excuse for kisses
in the summer
boys that rain You flesh'd girl, You peel these grapes
and wait for rested seers, stranger than the forest father coffee
rinds on shores and lovers
quicker than your heart can trot I hope you know,
Behind these cloven felts
the trees had sun
and all the arms of fallen cards that Leave away
there fallen rhymes on sullen eyes and fill the rinds of hungry
latest stomachs rise
The mezzanine,
my growing
Kitchen's wounds that call For many salt
I move not time
that Come my lodgings never home
but wait as i
the land in waste its very self-confusing word that wait to
grow With a higher voice
My little girl
Who argue not and wince their given oaths
of playing cards,

we argue
as we grow
the thoughts of girls that plucked the water sit and ask
with I,
The arms appraised
Who am I?
To argue on these spells that bind And who is he?
And what do we see, but fallen change, the pasture's honey
and the bees,
Alone and taught
The very weeds
and Growing wilting knives that bleed No more than friend
to me
I plead
to blindest natured
Never seen,
The significance of these seeds
Is that really me
I scatter
Like the lips that part their fat trovai and spell
The chosen course that pressed the swollen glands that very
sigh the weight of fall and winter lie
and burdened this
What is this hand-awakened earth
Too heavy for the honest man,
The grief the tongue will come with me,
like blood that asks,
in droplets mankind's peace is dressed in sweets
And waits for me
may all that come
the greyest matter
newest of the somnolencent Music,

Clang like Arab wives
the softest blue
The newest voyage gave me pride, I draw from you the
tones of
Very thorns that driven
Every sting,
The mouths of very tulips open everything that moves and
bear the wait to see
You gentlemen,
I circle long it cannot be The change of stolen lips exchange
refuse to fall
and waiver color
Lips like wistful balance fall The Keys as parted black Divide
on part'd moments exchanging god
I am, power
I dry the mind the drown Exchange and given rain
The songs of fluid planes
that Rise its base of every sect Inside the breach of door
that pollen
welcome,
call of floating airs of hell, The scenic bodies Venetian Firm
That marbled very nature Lie
with friend despise the eye That giveth flight
the second time that ask I float As fecund as a second
stomach, Nature's basest when it stands erect
On dorment grasses fleetest Jump'd feet,
Like younger bitter lust
The sensual
as industry
that Given flight
and mired in
The Spired

in the wave'd
waited for the plum'd light Inspired in your wave, You call
them lies.
The third if come as deep as sadness when it cries
of honey gold And appetite
The paper of thy plated
Lay
in coax'd threats Misunderstood
like mountain wrote with attitude
and flying dogs
And raining cats
that charm the somme,
the titan and the sleeping vow that pays the price
for withered vines
the sun can,
if given his day,
And if I were to say
no,
let up don't bother me
I have the scene and it was read
For the life of me, this voice is (is what it is) going on
The sun without hear,
Like a boy without his legs A thought without its rays As
strong as it is strong
As it is meant to be
the place where all the boys suppose'd are to Run
Better to fall over lies, Than to rest over your skin
as much as talks the sun

* * *

Like flowers red your feet Get lied for sullen tramples Sting
like pondered
what a happy scale to trust That Nature's reasons blind
Usurped as I that calls
that canted leave their very branches sob
Pluck away like flesh the color money confess
that you deserve me come a man that be As quick
as he is small,
to find It's merely growing Deaf And then they sparkle
Lost of marks of frostbit
suns and kin that
gaze and give you
as it said
The wandered
Come and lay with me the matching stars
as primes
at times I had them
Pruned and hearted,
adjusted in my very stomach
Churned like mountain milk in church,
desires that had lost
And with a vow of what
From plates retrieve the host
in homes that odd the argued
tongue to lasting wilts of wolven grief
The liar
and the dart that encore
holes in oceans
sounds the forest taken voyage
Emma can you pass this song test
Laugh with dinnered sounds you friend I watch from here
the sun of suns as you embark'd

again another letter
sent like fire flushing spring
I talk to sleeping
and to rest
You only say,
while turning wrists,
these moors they change
And given skin to me
It seems
under my weather jacket Emma,
wears the hide of luscious seas,
I sun with all my money
drown in all my sancti
mon' the frail
as jokes that look for meeting ends
Violent truths I've never written Given names,
I rose in books of
hollow idols,
Grown in every buildings
where the panels and the baskets of adopted flowers
green and chided youth and age'd pollen chose to charm like
thorns the little
flower
What a stomping monster
promise I'm as young as youth that livid longer, In my
burrowed hands
my little sun and daughter,
Come at once and read like pages
Numbered
driven Minutes session's halter
All the things I've seen
entire Sadness

as the very mode
of pleated armour
I love forever,
love my rhyme as I
As if it were to soirée
moss that grows
in shades
without me
curs'ed as
your words
that earn the sponge for dirty bodies Yougen, earthen,
ruddy,
Learning all your instrumental
crows and songbirds
Fabled honey Locust
all my reading tablets
I've seen all of your boys Imagined time that christen Dove is
what's this
Basins deeds that salted pointed fingers wounded Stirr'd all
my all's forgotten Is it Emma
say it's certain
tribes that centry spines the guard of spears of falling wits
and shoulders
promenade as gentlemen
I promise Turn my head to iris
open as the Irish flowers,
Mountains and their lost belongings,
Queen and consort eyes that color
Stolen from dusk
reason
wait like water
words to pardon.

To come upon a thing and faulter
Buzzing noises helicopters
newest source of springs and wells of water
Pulled to earth as this destruction as your blush as traits of
sweets of sticky chocolate
fingers
mark the brails of youth forgotten
Work into the sun you people
lie so flush and rise like idol flesh under the married dusk of
ribs and candy cotton,
Half of Aram his begotten,
Stranded as the shores of autumn
once my mother,
Tied as shoulders
beating hearts that hold the sinew,
And still I learn you,
Every note I plunder
scars and insert clothing,
Sounds that thread the yellow gold that bronze your nostrils,
yelling mothers,
Love for more than years I've waited,
Now for now it is a window,
Potted plants and seated hardwood,
Sounding out the pairs of vowels,
Waiting out your kinder garten,
Fallen as thyself the marksmen,
Permitting time to bleed my nature,
Carnal wishes selfish daughter
Give my life
for yours is longer
You're as good as books and had you brace
A spine as mine

in honey bronze as wide as teeth,
that pardon me
a name like star that stands the sun
with skinny ankles Father's wait
for sons as wade
before its white
My fingers swim
in up stream's Read
that first was lost in wetter mouths these spiders lie,
And had she nest
she would have wound
It would have heard

* * *

She would have caught
of skin and lint these emblems tie The rhyme of fish
the cause of space
the breath the time.
Press your cause
You finer sift the gold
From silt
the March of muds,
You idol dawn had found their god
In present huts have known your name,
From little rhymes of fluted tufts of ancient grain,
The mystics said to turn these eyes
To wake to cold and green
would be to see the sun
to mount in greedy eyes the mark of youth and float
It wandered in its shoal a broach for smaller children the
death of birth, the start of church.

worst than all the dreams of coal The breach of foals
your stomach grows
With luck your day that space
as snow
indoors, you wait,
The girl with candid
Light that feet It Dance
that turn their wit into things that melt
that fall for sons
the girls that Emma Boys
are cries on mountain's men
That large that girl a yes
and there are light
As stupid rhymes
As made to climb
in frozen air the glittered snow and wine and borrowed time
the sleets of hair.
I read a poem the last of youth
That found to be in later years The look of all that faulter's
fair
that fish of life
that frenzy Swarms the honey dew on lapse of water seeds
Appoint with colored wheel
The painting scheme,
I learn of letters, alphabets,
The turn of strands of amulets, and stolen luck,
If it were May,
I heard that there were music
the come a'front in dark
that if they played
On ears that not one more of word of girls that make their
name in wooden carved

Had earth but numbered
Watched as I in years
that shone With calloused eyes
the spoken page of youth,
The sun that bleeds in sweat
and climbs the trees,
and looks for ways
to think of you,
if spring would come again,
The Emma's eyes, In hearts that band Unflinching
pride
To shine again, To give me rise I've seen again
Unreal it said.
That Deserve'd sun that came On backs of pale
the soldiers Had
it guard that stand at tall at odds The cops and robbers
children's Fairy tails and marks of worn'ed Childhood shoes
on mark,
That talk of weary faulted flight, The time had come,
The sun had talked.
It was just then,
The sons that did as hired do, And Wait for sounds that
drink The wine,
that wait for song,
I'm fourth and fifth,
There's pause,
I guess
I guess

* * *

It's Emma's song,

Breath with me the light of ancient's Nobles fought, at once
my father grand,
With bandoliers,
Em have ever you
sat by the mouths of lakes that made upon the broach, My
had the forest come upon a tuft of grass,
As had the sun but one as Emma,
Loves her throngs of loves her naught,
Pulled apart like favorites tied Undid the shoes
that fish and fall.
Stick around the longer suns that ride the wave,
Commercials share a gait
On skin and air,
And pause the very breath
Of breaks,
To write the tongue might lay
The age of eight,
To pick a fight with the season's name for girls and boys, All
were fair game,
All were the fists as fly as love was lost
whats fair?
What's yours is mine
Emma lone as blank as broken
walk for house,
aligned with stripes,
With light that what for naught The nails at post
That will not say, a feist in child,
That reads as book that fond as wide As black and white
as eyes of swirling sweets
surprise
The chase of suns,
To clear the sweeps of brooms, And all of light,

Kick up in spec of dust may hide your flight,
My Parted
Bon good morn the light, The Em as one
as good as mine,
As I'm to I,
As old as women's broom
I crane my back
With grinning frame
and parse the ground with a pruning eye,
I work for Light, I wait for you

* * *

I had said that the sun had its third trimester, or it would have had its day, I keep them like the hours grown. I live in words of bellicose and French I say, the parts of noble oak. Cut into the slivers to be frayed over again.

Spaced without consideration, I came back to look to gawk, to manicure over the scuffs. The girl whose name is Emma, braids or parts her hair, but only in the middle of her eyes could ever see it. Funny and young with the confusion of youth. I carry my book and walk as if they're heavy

Hi, I am charmed to meet you, as I had on the reach of muskets been, I'm late to class and bind my notes in granite.

The nerve of them to mix these textures, the profundity of nature to have saturated me in rings. I grow into the fields anything more for you, I've learned to speak as my nectar grows a fluid question. Heart of hearts. I breath in this gymnasium enclosed in rib bones and milk and missing all but my needed fort. I speak like I attract nothing yet writers stare at me as if I have a domain. They call it wisdom. I pet like a foreign culture that would have eaten off me. I was once not as sharp as I'm used to.

Anything more as sharp as once a dullard I hide in all my crossing the most lavender of notes, tied upon the back of me, the dress I promenade within my tails.

It was nice until it left. And little more over the shoulders fell like the fluke of a crushed bands

Nice hair was it made it to be known. Nice eyes. It would be a shame if I saw them again. You first girl because it has to know rebellion. Until next time.

* * *

Emma had you come again, good morning as if one a sentence passed the test, I hid from thee like shyest girls the given cheek, who do I fair a bloody world, lament the older sun where did I come, what had I earned that you could stand the broach of youthful.

This is my final place to rest remember sun the light that fell to grow like tree a boy to man, to spirit thought and light the bear that wave that wolves of roam, the pianist that sings and writes is she delight the newest lands to land to pains the light over the newest dough.

The fall that I behind, I mind my newest place and fall upon
this early story,
may I know the sun as us,
as soon as night would come
I wait in the air for the sound of living things
the Emma grow with you, having known a loss of
wonder once
as a wheel of enterprise

another fable cry
again,
not were alone this time the sun that looks to be the son
again,
the last again to grow with thee another day.

* * *

The atmosphere is not perfume, before they made a motor, a decent one anyway, the shade had come in interruptions that were in between the stutter and breath. Any one of these things can know who I am. That there is an I

He knew what all the things know in order to live, that if you stop this tribe of moving time, in it, you will rest and move and reckon with the self.

And then you will do something with yourself, your body on your belly that is, and what to do with colors after that

There is always this thing to ascertain after it is said, with two fingers, there was something gone between the two.

And because we continue, because this is more of what is left, that is I remain with the flat land and all that does breathe in it, Lying like an egg in infinity I marvel at its nesting edges, and go on within, with words no bigger than science to obtain myself.

And what about the shrill of this glance of what was me? Not so much a question between an ounce of steel and a catacomb,

Man in contact with me, a note of A in my clothes, and in my madness, he says:

I am yet to fall in love with it,

I am here and it never happened.

I

So far as my ears are soft to collide like green on the rocks
What he does with his spirit in the space between his nose
and arms,
the I that is, as tall as a budding tree
I lose my self and speak of pride.

II

To speak of a man that prances in the sound of water
until it is warm and running, with beads that lean on back
legs and ornery mouths so feed.
This is what I heard of talking, and the blankets and the
fondness, and to ask of a book any more unwritten than now
is to hear it misspelled such enough that it is content with
what it is, a light between the how so that breaks the edges
and demands its place among the living.
Urge and urge and light a fire between my hearth, and out
the name kings that spar with me
Tearing off their embers,
growing like the sun,
furtive as a word
entrenched Haughty, unsure, eloquent, furious that you had
loved me
growing into beams from nothing
dawning that it holds its place to know the me and you

The first horse that shook its head and learned that it is so we
stand

III

New and sweet is my hide,
new and unridden,
even as a soul waiting his turn,
ides and tufts of hair in march diving through my ages,
drunken as my fingers,
feeding as a menace this stout equanimity, menacing my
shoulders and admiring the flight
I welcome every damned remembrance of me
As they speak about heart, and loath under my fingers, and
break like teeth under lips
Satisfied with dancing and brooding in the wind, Hugging
and loving,
Treading in my bed with its faces
with warning it its eyes
I see it at a distance as if it was an onyx, emblazoned with the
names of stones, heavy as a snowfall
I gallant with my early self, unafraid to speak for me, and
dress me, And give me money,
and be my hand,
and break did this foot to fall like brothers in the news

IV

Remitting as I held the rains, that turn like beggars
and pour man in my mouth The envy of cities that wait
Given to my eyes

a walk against the bigshots and the footmen Hauling carts of
water
Days after men were dry
dazed and amused at the curvature of the world, it won this
war of plaid buck stately and ornament, authors in their
cannons that argue
None of them can get me

V

I wait for you my god, as the sun did shine in my soul,
I abase myself
In ether!
Prance with me in this atmosphere
As you once did, roiling in perfume
I dress like the sparkle of money
as an emperor with a woman he loves,
Willing to do ill
Stiff with words of discontent
The creation writhes teeming with the air beneath me
I tighten and swell full of the leech
answering in the garden with a worm for my pen,
grown that I am,
a language that is lost like the tears of hares
and given to the blacks
Tenderly I love the ocean,
with ivory for the corners of its mouth, speaking in tongues
foraging for its notes
Drooping with its young age
currents of yes it was on the floorboards.
I love all of your love,

in and out,
tripe within the grown it of the earth,
In my stomach it rises like the wild fire,
bleeding with the tenderness that saunters on its mothers
neck,
Without repetition the earth lay bare
like flecks of varnished wood,
Held out in its hands silk worms in all the matter, shouting
at its lap
Take my line,
I will sprout again on the cuff,
As a blind man drooping in his loins,
As a horse and child heavy with his coin,
Still god, still gallant,
As all of creation my sister Forever and ever, amen.